Life in  *Times*

Home & School

Neil Morris

Belitha Press

First published in the UK in 1999 by
Belitha Press Limited, London House,
Great Eastern Wharf, Parkgate Road,
London SW11 4NQ

This edition first published in 2000

ISBN 1 84138 148 9 (paperback)
ISBN 1 85561 888 5 (hardback)

British Library Cataloguing in Publication Data
for this book is available from the British Library.

Series editor: Honor Head
Series designer: Jamie Asher
Picture researcher: Diana Morris
Consultant: Sallie Purkis

Printed in Singapore

Picture credits
Hulton Getty: back cover b, 4c, 5b, 6, 9b, 11c, 12, 13t, 14,
15t, 16, 17c, 18, 20, 21c, 23t, 23c, 23b, 24, 25t, 26, 27c,
27b, 28.

Public Record Office: front cover, back cover t, 1, 2, 3, 4b,
5t, 5c, 7t, 7c, 7b, 8, 9t, 10, 11t, 11b, 13b,15c, 15b, 17t,
17b, 19t, 19b, 21t, 21b, 22, 25b, 27t, 29t, 29c, 29b.

Words in **bold** are in the glossary on pages 30 and 31.

CONTENTS

INTRODUCTION

In Victorian times, life was hard for working-class parents and their children. The whole family often had to live in a couple of small rooms. There was usually no running water and no indoor lavatory. For the better-off middle classes, the situation was very different. Their big houses usually had a drawing room, dining room, **parlour** and kitchen, with a spacious nursery for the children.

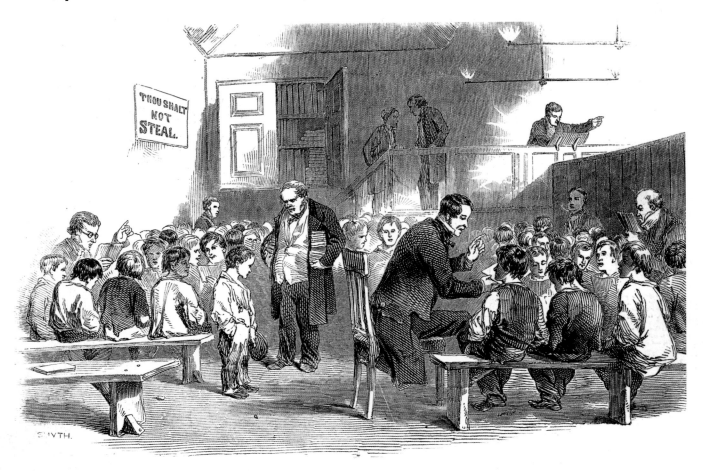

We use the word Victorian to describe the time when Queen Victoria was on the British throne. Born in 1819, Victoria was the only child of Edward, the fourth son of King George III, and Victoria Maria Louisa, the daughter of a German duke. She became queen in 1837, and three years later married Albert, a German prince. They had nine children before Albert died in 1861. Victoria ruled for almost 64 years, longer than any other British monarch. She died in 1901, at the age of 81.

Home life changed for Victorians of all classes with the development of important medical discoveries and improvements in public health. Many thousands of people died in outbreaks of cholera and other deadly diseases, before **reformers** brought about the building of proper drains and sewers in all town areas, whether rich or poor. By the end of the Victorian era people were living longer, healthier lives in better living conditions.

Before 1870, many children did not go to school at all. This was because they needed to work to help support the family. Then the law was changed so that all children had to go to school. Well-off parents had always sent their sons away to boarding schools, while their daughters were usually taught at home by a **governess**. In all Victorian schools, teaching was more formal than it is today and discipline was strict.

MIDDLE-CLASS HOMES

The Victorian **middle classes** lived in large, comfortable houses. Many of these are still standing today, though some have been divided into smaller flats or offices. The houses usually had three floors, with extra attic rooms and a large basement.

The kitchen was in the basement. On the ground floor were the dining room and parlour, or sitting room. Visitors were often entertained in the drawing room, on the first floor. The second storey was taken up with bedrooms, and servants lived at the top of the house in small attic rooms. Most middle-class homes had an indoor lavatory, but chamber pots were kept in the bedrooms for use during the night.

Most of the furniture was made of dark, heavy wood such as mahogany and oak. Well-off families liked to fill their rooms with ornaments, paintings, candlesticks and clocks. They also liked everything to be kept free of dust and dirt, so there was plenty of cleaning for the family's servants. The man of the house generally went out to work during the day, while his wife stayed at home or visited other ladies' houses for tea.

► *A mother and her young family spend time together in the drawing room. This was a comfortable room for sitting in and spending leisure time, as well as for entertaining guests. The name of the room was originally withdrawing room because it was where women would withdraw, or go, after dinner. It had nothing to do with the sort of drawing that this family are doing. Drawing was thought to be a useful accomplishment, or social skill, especially for young ladies. So too was piano-playing, which was very popular in Victorian times, and a drawing room always contained a piano.*

RIPPINGILLE'S PATENT Oil Warming STOVES
The Best in the World.

FOR SALE HERE

◀ *Victorian homes had no central heating, and most were kept warm in winter by coal fires. There was a fireplace in most rooms, and coal had to be added all the time to keep the fire burning. This advertisement of 1894 offers a new form of heating – stoves that burn oil instead of coal. Everyone looks very comfortable, but by today's standards most houses then were cold and draughty.*

▼ *Victorian water closets, or lavatories. The tank above the toilet contained water, which came down the pipe to flush the toilet when the user pulled the chain. Victorians liked to have fancy designs for everything, and these lavatories are in the shape of a shellfish (left) and a Greek* **vessel** *(right). These were a great luxury, and poorer homes had 'earth closets' in an outside shed, which they often had to share between families.*

▲ *This luxury bathroom has an early form of shower. When the bather pulled the chain, water simply dropped out of the container to give a quick shower. In houses without bathrooms, people bathed in tin tubs filled with hot water from the kitchen. In better-off homes, the tubs would be carried to a bedroom and put next to a roaring fire in winter.*

BACK-TO-BACK

Housing conditions for workers and their families were often very poor. People who moved to new factory towns from the country were used to small cottages, but the cottages usually had some space around them. In towns, most houses were built in terraces, or rows, joined at the back by small yards. Instead of indoor lavatories, people used outdoor 'privies' above **cesspits** that were shared by several houses. The open drains helped to spread disease.

Victorian families were large and so houses were overcrowded. Children often slept all together in one large bed, in the same room as their parents. People usually had to fetch water from a tank or **standpipe** in the street. From the 1860s well-meaning businessmen put money into better houses for working families in London and other large cities.

Some factory owners, like the Lever Brothers who made soap, went even further. In 1888 they built a whole village for their workers in north-west England. The houses in Port Sunlight all had small kitchens, called sculleries, as well as their own bathrooms.

◄ *This dingy room in east London was home to a tailor and his whole family. They all helped make uniforms for the British army, for which they received very little money. The house was in a poor district of London, where water for up to 15 houses came from one tap in a dirty corner of the street.*

▲ This row of **almshouses** was built in 1849 for poor, elderly and **infirm** citizens of Tooting, in south London. The project was used as a model for other areas. There were 40 houses, and each had an entrance passage, parlour, bedroom and kitchen. They had no bathroom, but there was a separate wash house with running hot and cold water, as well as a laundry.

▼ These blocks of flats, built in London in 1879, were described as 'model **artisans'** dwellings'. They were built by a **housing association** and rented out to skilled workers, such as printers and plumbers, and their families. The idea was that the **investors** who put up the money for the project should let them as cheaply as possible so that they made just a small profit. The three blocks housed 2000 tenants.

UPSTAIRS, DOWNSTAIRS

Some working-class families employed a young relative as a maid. She helped the family with daily household chores and in return she was given **board and lodging**. In larger households, servants spent much of their time in the kitchen or servants' hall 'below stairs' or in the basement. The family members lived upstairs and rarely went downstairs.

Many middle-class households had a cook who could make elaborate dinners. She often had a helper to prepare the ingredients. If she was less qualified, she was known as a 'plain' cook. A parlour maid laid the table, acted as a waitress during mealtimes and helped generally with other duties. A housemaid spent most of her time cleaning. Usually, she was not much older than the family's children.

Rich people also had gardeners and footmen. They employed a **butler** to take charge of all the other male servants, and a **housekeeper** to watch over the female staff. A coachman looked after and drove the master's horse-drawn carriage. Because most jobs had to be done by hand rather than with the help of a machine, there was a lot of housework to do. Servants were generally given decent accommodation and good food and clothes, as well as their pay.

All the meals were prepared in the kitchen, using a large stove that was heated by burning coal. The stove was called a range, or a kitchener, and it was fitted with ovens, plate-warmers and water-heaters. This one is being used to advertise a quick-boiling kettle, which the cook is looking very pleased with. Servants polished the range regularly to keep it clean and its fire was lit early every morning. Ashes from the fire fell into the grate at the front, which had to be emptied.

FURNITURE SHINE

Far Superior TO ORDINARY FURNITURE CREAMS.

Can be used for the MOST DELICATE FURNITURE.

SOLE PROPRIETORS **T STOTHERT & Cº LTD** — WHOLESALE DRUGGISTS. BLACKBURN

◄ There was a lot of furniture for the servants to dust and polish. This advertisement of 1894 shows one of the many brands of furniture cream that were available. Books and household manuals were full of recipes for polishes and creams that could be made at home.

▼ Very large houses had separate laundries and laundry maids to deal with all the washing. By the end of the Victorian age, some households had replaced washing tubs with hand-operated washers such as this one. It worked by turning the big handle. The washing was then put through the silver-coloured wringer on the other side, which squeezed out a lot of the water.

BROOKE'S SOAP MONKEY BRAND

WON'T WASH CLOTHES

MAKES BRIGHT REFLECTIONS

▲ This cleaning soap apparently worked so brilliantly that we can see a reflection of the maid in all the pots and pans. The row of bells above the door at the top right were operated from different rooms in the house, so that maids could be called when they were needed upstairs.

FAMILY LIFE

Working people had to spend so much of their day earning a living that there was not much time left for anything else. Home life was mainly made up of eating and sleeping, so that parents and children were all fit and ready for the next day's work.

Middle-class family life was very different. It was ordered and followed a predictable pattern. Victorian fathers were very much the head of their family. They gave orders and expected to be obeyed by their wife, children and servants. Until the law was changed in 1882, a husband owned all his wife's money and property. Most men spent little time with their children, but took a great interest in their behaviour and progress.

Middle-class mothers didn't go out to work and they had servants to do their housework and cooking, so we might think that they led a lazy life. But they had plenty to do managing the servants, planning meals and generally running the household. In their spare time, women would pay calls on other ladies and go shopping.

◀ *This illustration, which was drawn in 1876, shows a very happy picture of a Victorian family. They are all reading books and magazines, and the younger members are looking at picture books. Since Victorian times were well before the days of radio or television, people of all ages spent a great deal of time reading. Books, **periodicals** and newspapers gave people information and entertainment.*

► *This Victorian family was photographed having tea. They look very still and posed because they were probably not used to having their photograph taken. Also, people had to stay very still for a long time while they were being photographed so that the picture did not blur. Mealtimes gave families the opportunity to spend time together and talk. Meals were always taken seated around a table. Grace, a short prayer of thanksgiving to God, was usually said before the meal.*

◄ *Many Victorian families liked to keep their own record of births, marriages and deaths. This register includes space for the dates on which babies were admitted to the Christian church by being **baptized** and **christened**, and later when older children were **confirmed**. The married couple's 'issue' meant their children. Such registers often appeared in family Bibles, which were handed down through the generations.*

IN THE NURSERY

Victorian parents generally believed in the saying that children 'should be seen and not heard'. The nursery, or children's room, was usually at the top of the house, so that any noise during the day would not disturb the adults. Children would learn and play in the day nursery, and sleep in the next-door night nursery.

In well-off families, young children were looked after by a full-time **nanny**, who was called nurse and known by her surname – Nurse Jones, for example. The nanny had complete control over the children in her care, acting in many ways like most parents today. She helped the children dress and eat, played with them, took them for walks, read to them, bathed them and put them to bed. Most children felt very close to their nanny, who would often stay with one family for her whole working life.

Most mothers spent only a short time with their children each day. Fathers saw their children briefly before they went to bed. Victorian parents felt that this was the right way to bring up children and it gave the mother the time to run the home efficiently.

◄ *This photograph was probably specially taken for the family album. Mothers whose husbands could afford it had a* **nursemaid** *as well as a nanny to look after their babies and run the nursery.*

◄ This child is playing with a Noah's ark. The pairs of model animals could be put into the ark, as in the Bible story, so that they were safe from the great flood. This was the only toy children were allowed to play with on Sundays. Only rich parents could afford to buy such toys and most other Victorian toys were home-made.

STEPS TO READING.

BY N. DALE.

WITH PICT- 'URES BY WAL- TER CRANE

LONDON: J.M.DENT.&C?

► This small girl takes her first 'steps to reading'. Walter Crane (1845-1915) was one of the most popular illustrators of children's books. He worked on several books that were intended to teach children to read, including this one by Nellie Dale.

▼ These ABC picture cards, designed to teach children the letters of the alphabet, were printed in 1885. Some of the names of animals and objects are quite difficult words to read. Alphabet books were popular in Victorian times.

ACORN ARK ANTELOPE ANEMONE AXE.

BLUE-BELL BAT BLACKBIRD BRAMBLE BALL

CROCUS COCK CATERPILLAR CUP COBWEB

DOG DUC DAIRY-MA DAIS

L GOOSE OSLING SEBERRY

HARE HOOP HAWK HEDGEHOG

INK IVY ICICLE JACKDAW JAM

JAM

KEY KID KITTEN KNITTIN

EARLY SCHOOLS

For the first half of Queen Victoria's reign, there was no national system of education. In those days many children from working families did not go to school at all, mainly because they spent most of their time at work. Some rich people believed this was right, because schooling might lead poor young people to disagree with their 'elders and betters'.

The free schools that did exist were run by churches and charities. Church Sunday schools had started before Victorian times, and their example inspired the setting up of **ragged schools** in the 1840s. The name for these schools came from the ragged appearance of their poor pupils. The great reformer Anthony Ashley Cooper, 7th Earl of Shaftesbury (1801-85), was chairman of the Ragged Schools Union.

Some children went to dame schools, so called because they were run by elderly ladies. Others received basic schooling in the **workhouse** where they lived or the factory where they worked. Most schools concentrated on teaching the three Rs: reading, writing and arithmetic.

▲ *At the beginning of the Victorian age, many church schools had one huge classroom with hundreds of pupils. The teacher stood or sat at the front of the class and was helped by a number of monitors, who looked after a few rows of pupils each. The monitors were older students who passed on the lessons they learned from the teacher. The kites and hoops hanging from the ceiling were used as rewards for good work.*

► This ragged school opened in a poor district of London in 1843. The streets around the school were full of gangs of thieves. At first the school opened only on Sundays and had 70 pupils in summer. But in winter this figure doubled, with street children looking for shelter from the cold. By the end of the 1860s there were over 600 ragged schools across the country.

◄ This workshop was the **industrial school** upstairs at the Brook Street Ragged School. The room was turned into a **dormitory** for the boys at night. The boys were able to support themselves by the work they did there. Some pupils managed to save up enough money to buy a boat ticket and **emigrate** to America.

► This schoolroom was run by a boys' home. Here boys learned to read and write as well as being taught tailoring, shoemaking and carpentry. There was a separate home for girls. Another charitable children's home was opened in 1858 by Dr Thomas John Barnardo. It was the first of many.

BOARD SCHOOLS

In 1870, a new Education Act was passed by parliament. The new law said that all children should go to school from the age of five to ten. School Boards were set up all over the country, and they opened new schools in areas where there was not already a church school. At first the Board Schools were not free. Parents had to pay a few pence each week, and this was enough to keep the children of poorer families away.

If parents wanted their children to learn more than reading, writing, arithmetic and religion, they usually had to pay extra. Board School teachers had to be able to teach many different subjects, including history, but the three Rs were considered most important. The children often copied what was written on the blackboard, or they learned by reciting tables or lists in chorus.

Even before the 1870 Education Act, the government sent round school inspectors to check on the progress of schools, teachers and pupils. Pupils had to pass tests before they could move up to the next standard, or class.

▼ *The girls' class in a Board School, in 1876. As with earlier, different types of school, boys and girls were taught separately. If the schoolroom was mixed, they still sat apart. Girls had school-mistresses and boys had schoolmasters. In larger Board Schools, there were separate entrances and yards for boys and girls. These girls are copying on to their slates from the teacher's blackboard.*

►Some School Boards had a course of **housewifery** lessons as part of the girls' **syllabus**. Pupils brought in their own clothes and took them home again washed and ironed. They also learned how to light a fire, make a bed, lay a dinner table and sweep a room. The Board said that these were the 'chief items of work in a working man's home'.

▼ This Board School in Derbyshire was new when it was photographed in 1880. Many Victorian schools were built to a similar design, and some are still in use today.

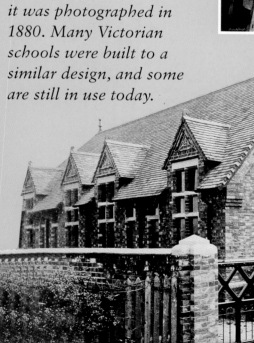

WORK AND SCHOOL

In 1880, the school-leaving age was raised from 10 to 13. This caused problems for the many parents who relied on their children's income, so 10 to 13 year-olds were allowed to work part-time. This meant that some children arrived at school very tired. They might work from five in the morning on a farm or in a factory, and then go back to work after school until 10 o'clock at night.

In 1891 schools were at last made free and gradually many parents began to take pride in their children's learning. Some lessons became more practical. Science was often taught through an 'object lesson'. Objects such as snails, rocks, or lumps of sugar were placed in front of the class, so that pupils could look at them while the teacher read out lists of facts about them.

Young children learned to write the letters of the alphabet by using a sand tray. They drew the letters in the sand with their fingers. They learned to write whole words on **slates**, scratching on them with sharpened slate pencils. The slates could be wiped clean and used over and over again. Older children learned to use pen and ink by copying handwriting.

▶ *Combining work and school was hard for many children. This girl looks very tired, and she was probably not attending to her work properly. The machinery in this cotton mill could be very dangerous, and the girl might injure herself or lose her job.*

20

◀ Certificates helped to make pupils and their parents feel that there was a real point to going to school. Registers were kept very thoroughly, including notes on punctuality and comments on behaviour. Inspectors also checked on schools to make sure that pupils were taught properly and that certificates were awarded correctly.

◀ Children sat in rows of desks with the teacher at the front. Pupils were not allowed to leave their desk without permission from the teacher. The whole class usually worked on the same thing, in this case copying a drawing of a fly. Teachers were generally much tougher than they are today, finding things wrong rather than praising a good effort.

▶ Wealthy parents could buy their children books and kits, so that they could learn more at home. This chemistry set was on sale in 1897. While this boy was doing his experiments at home, other children of his age were at work, helping to support their family.

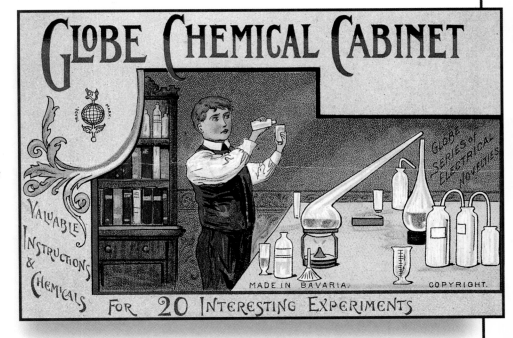

GLOBE CHEMICAL CABINET

GLOBE SERIES OF ELECTRICAL NOVELTIES

VALUABLE INSTRUCTIONS & CHEMICALS

MADE IN BAVARIA.   COPYRIGHT.

FOR 20 INTERESTING EXPERIMENTS

PRIVATE EDUCATION

The sons of rich families were generally sent away to boarding school at the age of 12. Some of these **public schools**, which were actually expensive private schools, were founded centuries before the Victorian age. Teaching concentrated on the classical subjects of Latin and Greek. Senior boys had a lot of power over their juniors, who had to 'fag' for them by cleaning their shoes, fetching things and running errands.

The style of some public schools was changed by Thomas Arnold (1795-1842), who was headmaster of Rugby School when Victoria came to the throne. He introduced a proper system of **prefects** among the older boys, as well as new subjects such as French and modern history. His methods were described in 1857 in a book called *Tom Brown's Schooldays* by Thomas Hughes, one of Arnold's former pupils.

There were some public day schools for girls by the 1870s, but girls were mainly educated at home by a governess. Many rich Victorians thought it a waste of money to educate their daughters.

▼ *The new part of Dulwich College, south of London, as seen in 1879. The original college, or school, opened in 1619, and the New College was built in 1870. It was designed in an Italian style by the famous English architect Sir Charles Barry, who had already rebuilt the Houses of Parliament in London. The boys in the foreground are playing cricket.*

▲ The upper school and school yard at Eton College, in 1890. This famous school in Windsor, Berkshire, was founded in 1440 by King Henry VI. Eton was originally for 90 pupils, but had become much bigger by Victorian times. Today there are more than 1200 boys at Eton.

▼ Cricket and other team sports were very important at Victorian public schools. Teachers thought that they helped build up the character of the players. Cricketers had to learn to obey their captain, play as a team member, respect their opponents, and learn to lose without complaining.

◄ The governess spent a lot of time with the children in her charge. She had probably been educated at home herself. In the nineteenth century private teaching was the only paid employment that many people thought suitable for a young lady. Most governesses earned up to £45 a year.

HOSPITAL CARE

During the first half of the nineteenth century hospitals were not very clean places. Doctors and surgeons hardly cleaned their instruments or their clothes and aprons. They had no idea that they were spreading germs and probably causing the infections that killed some of their patients.

In 1865 Joseph Lister (1827-1912), a surgeon at Glasgow Royal Infirmary, started to try and stop wounds becoming infected after operations. He realized that new methods were needed during operations. He **sterilized** all his surgical instruments to make them free of germs, and invented a **carbolic** spray which helped to kill germs in the air. Fewer people died in Lister's ward, and gradually hospitals everywhere started following his methods.

Hospital conditions were also improved by Florence Nightingale (1820-1910), who led a party of nurses to the **Crimean War** in 1854. She worked hard to change the terrible conditions in the British army hospitals, and every night went around her wards to comfort her patients. She became known as the Lady with the Lamp.

▼ *Lister's carbolic spray is being used during this operation, for which the surgeons are wearing their ordinary clothes. Before surgery, Lister's students used to joke, 'Let us spray'. The patient has been sent to sleep by an **anaesthetic** called chloroform. Queen Victoria used chloroform when she gave birth to her eighth child, which made it more popular with the general public.*

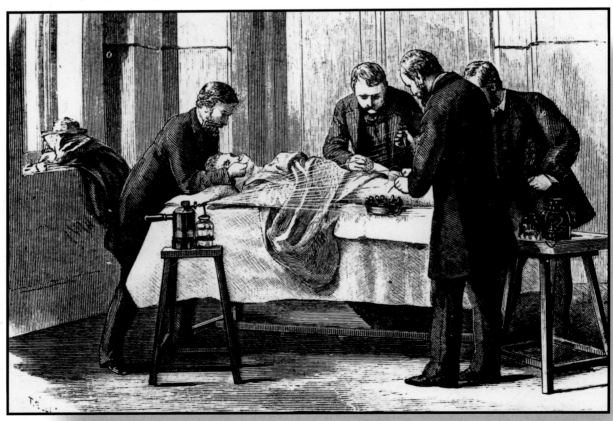

► In this photograph taken in 1886, Florence Nightingale (in the white shawl) is surrounded by nurses. After she returned from the Crimean War, she had started a campaign to train women as professional nurses. In 1860 she opened the Nightingale Training School for Nurses at St Thomas' Hospital in London. By the end of the century, many of her students were working in new, improved hospitals.

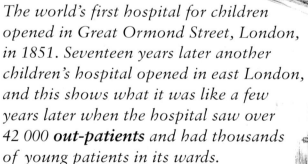

The world's first hospital for children opened in Great Ormond Street, London, in 1851. Seventeen years later another children's hospital opened in east London, and this shows what it was like a few years later when the hospital saw over 42 000 **out-patients** and had thousands of young patients in its wards.

MEDICAL TREATMENT

In the early 1800s doctors knew little about the real causes of many common illnesses. They could only offer simple remedies that were often useless. In any case, most people could not afford to visit a doctor because they had to pay for his services. They often tried to treat themselves, using traditional 'cures', such as eating live snails to treat tuberculosis. Many Victorians took the dangerous drug opium to ease pain, and some mothers even gave a form of the drug to their babies to stop them crying.

In Victorian times serious diseases included typhoid, typhus, diphtheria, tuberculosis and cholera. Most illness was caused by living in houses without proper drains or **sewers**, drinking dirty water or eating infected food. People feared cholera most, and in 1848 the disease killed 15 000 people in London. After another cholera outbreak in 1854, John Snow (1813-58) studied the way the disease seemed to be linked to water supplies. He discovered that it spread in drinking water that contained sewage. Dr Snow and others, such as the reformer Sir Edwin Chadwick (1800-90), persuaded the local authorities to look carefully at their water supplies. By 1900 Britain was covered by a huge network of new sewers and **water mains**.

▶ *Many new medicines and remedies were sold in Victorian times. Eno's 'fruit salt', a powder for upset stomachs, was one of the most successful. It was developed by James Crossley Eno (1828-1915) in his Newcastle **pharmacy**. It became so popular in the 1870s that Eno opened a small factory in London. He became very rich, but still wrote all his own advertisements. He donated money to Guy's Hospital and Dr Barnardo's children's homes.*

ENO
HEALTH'S MESSENGER

THE JEOPARDY OF LIFE IS IMMENSELY INCREASED without such a simple precaution as

It is not too much to say that merits have been published, tested and approved literally from pole to pole, and that its cosmopolitan popularity to-day presents one of the most sig illustrations of commercial enterprise to be found in trading records.

ENO'S "FRUIT SALT"

◄ *This illustration of a family doctor appeared in a periodical of 1880. An article stressed how hard doctors had to work. On most days the doctor held a free surgery for poor people from six to nine in the morning. From nine to two he saw his better-off, paying patients. Then a carriage took him on his rounds visiting sick people. At five he spent an hour writing letters, and from six to eight in the evening he saw patients referred to him by other doctors. At nine he visited patients who were critically ill. And when he got back home, there was often a telegram waiting to call him out again.*

► *A district vaccinator at work in 1871. Vaccination involved injecting people with a tiny amount of a disease so that they became immune to it without getting ill. This came into use in the late eighteenth century, and in Victorian times was increasingly used against smallpox, cholera and typhoid.*

► *Elizabeth Garrett Anderson (1836-1917) was not allowed to study at medical school because she was a woman. So she studied privately and passed the medical exams. In 1865 she was given a licence to practise and became the first qualified woman doctor in Britain. She then helped set up a hospital for women in London.*

ROYAL FAMILY

Princess Alexandrina Victoria was just a year old when her father died, and she was brought up by her mother and a German governess. Victoria enjoyed singing and dancing when she was little, and soon took to horseriding. Just after her 18th birthday her life changed dramatically when her uncle, King William IV, died. Victoria became Queen of the United Kingdom of Great Britain and Ireland and moved into Buckingham Palace.

She married Prince Albert three years later, and they had four sons and five daughters over the next 17 years. The queen's letters and diaries show her great love for her husband and children. Many stories about the royal family appeared in newspapers and magazines, and they won the respect and admiration of the people. This was important for the royal family, because the previous kings had not been very popular. The Queen had a very strong sense of duty, and her family became a model for the whole nation.

Albert died of typhoid in 1861, and Victoria never really recovered from her grief. She stopped attending social events and dressed in black for many years. Her children, grandchildren and great-grandchildren were very important to her. When she died in 1901, her eldest son became King Edward VII.

▶ Queen Victoria, Prince Albert and their children enjoy their Christmas tree in 1850. The tradition of decorating a tree for Christmas was brought to Britain by Prince Albert in the 1840s. He came from Coburg, in south Germany, where decorations and small toys were an important part of the Christmas festivities. The royal children were delighted with the idea, and paintings such as this one led others to follow the example. Before long, many British families had a Christmas tree at home.

► Balmoral Castle, near the banks of the River Dee in Scotland, where the Queen and her family spent many of their summer holidays. Victoria and Albert bought the **estate** in 1847, and replaced the original house with this large granite building. The Castle was finished in 1856, and Queen Victoria was always happy there. Queen Elizabeth II and the present royal family still regularly stay in the Castle.

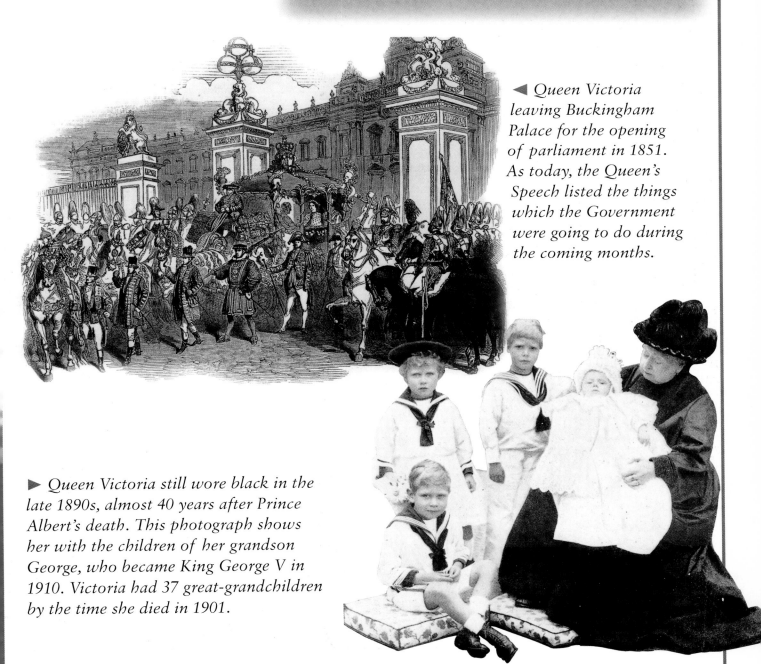

◄ Queen Victoria leaving Buckingham Palace for the opening of parliament in 1851. As today, the Queen's Speech listed the things which the Government were going to do during the coming months.

► Queen Victoria still wore black in the late 1890s, almost 40 years after Prince Albert's death. This photograph shows her with the children of her grandson George, who became King George V in 1910. Victoria had 37 great-grandchildren by the time she died in 1901.

Glossary

almshouse a house for poor people that is paid for by a charity.

anaesthetic a substance given to a patient so that they do not feel any pain.

artisan a skilled worker or craftsman.

baptize to admit a person into the Christian church.

board and lodging regular meals and a place to live.

butler the head man in charge of the other male servants, who also looks after the wine cellar and table cutlery.

carbolic a chemical used to kill germs.

cesspit an underground container that collects waste from lavatories.

christen to give a Christian name to a baby when he or she is baptized.

confirm to make an older child a member of the Christian church.

Crimean War the war of 1853-56 fought between Britain, France, Turkey and Sardinia on one side, and Russia on the other; it took place in a region of present-day Ukraine called Crimea.

dormitory a large sleeping room with many beds.

emigrate to leave your own country to go and live in another country.

estate a big area of land, usually with a large house in the middle.

governess a woman who is employed by a family to teach children at home.

housekeeper a woman in charge of all the other female servants.

housewifery the skills and work of looking after and running a house, especially as a housewife.

housing association an organization which builds or improves houses and flats so that they can be let to people at a fair rent.

income money earned by working.

industrial school a school with a workshop where young people were taught to make things.

infirm weak in health.

investor a person who puts money into a project in order to make a profit.

middle class people in a class of society which includes the families of professional and business workers, such as bankers, solicitors, doctors and office workers.

nanny a woman who is employed by a family to look after the young children.

nursemaid a woman who looks after a baby or a very young child.

out-patient someone who goes to a hospital for treatment but does not stay there overnight.

parlour a sitting room with comfortable chairs.

periodical a newspaper or magazine that comes out at regular intervals, usually weekly or monthly.

pharmacy a place where medicines and drugs are prepared and sold.

prefect a school pupil who is allowed to tell other, younger pupils what to do.

public school a private school, especially for boarders, that charges fees.

ragged school a free school for poor children.

reformer a person who tries to make improvements in people's lives.

sewer a large underground pipe that carries waste matter from homes.

slate a flat smooth plate of grey rock (also called slate), sometimes put in a wooden frame and used for writing on.

standpipe a pipe in the street with a tap, where people can collect water in buckets.

sterilize to make something free of germs.

surgeon a doctor who performs medical operations.

syllabus all the subjects studied at school.

vessel a container for liquids, like a large pot.

water main a large underground pipe that carries water.

workhouse a place where poor people received food and accommodation in return for work.

Index